Contents

Acknowledgements

Photographs
page 5 © 2003/plainpicture/Sperling, S./Alamy.com
page 6 © H. Armstrong Roberts/Corbis
page 8 © Ford Smith/Corbis
pages 11, 31 and 61 © Image Club
page 12 ©Bettmann/Corbis
page 22 © 2003/Rolf Richardson/Alamy.com
pages 26 and 52 Images kindly supplied by the Early Learning Centre
page 38 © Getty images/Stone
page 47 © 2003/Ian McKinnell/Alamy.com

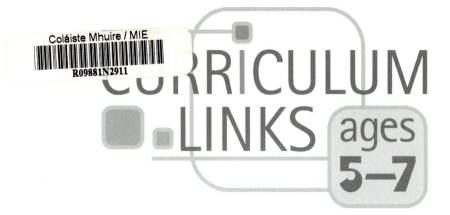

CURRICULUM
LINKS ages
5–7

Toys

Suzanne Kirk

Credits

Author
Suzanne Kirk

Editor
Roanne Charles

Assistant editor
Nina Bruges

Series designer
Lynne Joesbury

Designer
Catherine Mason

Illustrations
Debbie Clark

Cover photograph
© SODA

Photographic symbols
PE and history © Stockbyte.
Design & technology © Photodisc, Inc.

Published by Scholastic Ltd,
Villiers House,
Clarendon Avenue,
Leamington Spa,
Warwickshire
CV32 5PR
Printed by Bell & Bain Ltd, Glasgow
Text © Suzanne Kirk
© 2003 Scholastic Ltd
1 2 3 4 5 6 7 8 9   3 4 5 6 7 8 9 0 1 2

Visit our website at www.scholastic.co.uk

British Library Cataloguing-in-Publication Data
A catalogue record for this book is available from
the British Library.

ISBN 0-439-98439-4

Introduction

This book provides suggestions and activities covering separate areas of the curriculum that, as a whole, extend children's experience of toys. It raises their awareness of the characteristics of toys past and present and focuses their interest on puppets as a particular group of toys. These are used as inspiration for designing and making and for dance movements.

Toys brings together aspects of history, design and technology and the dance element of physical education. It will help you to present an interesting and relevant topic at Key Stage 1 over a number of weeks, enabling children to find out and learn about toys, particularly their structure and movement.

Generally, the activities in each section of Toys follow on progressively. The activities of section 3 build up to presenting toys as they are displayed in a museum, demonstrating the communication of information and ideas. In section 4, the children practise techniques that they will need during section 5 in which they design and make their own puppets. The dance activities provide a progressive sequence of imagination, ideas and practice that culminates in a performance of dance ideas.

What subject areas are covered?

This book covers the QCA Schemes of Work history unit 1, 'How are our toys different from those in the past?', design and technology unit 2B, 'Puppets', and dance activities unit 1 of physical education.

All children are fascinated by toys. They have their favourites of course, but are inquisitive about new and unusual toys, eager to investigate the latest invention or examine any new product. During this topic, children are encouraged to look closely at all kinds of toys, particularly puppets, identify their different parts, ask questions and make useful comparisons. Identifying differences and similarities between old

© 2003/plainpicture/Sperling, S./Alamy.com

and newer toys gives children a glimpse of the past and an appreciation of the childhood experiences of their parents and grandparents. In putting together a simple museum, the children learn an appealing visual way of communicating to others what they have learned about toys. They discuss ideas for designing and making a puppet, using techniques they have practised. Toys and puppets are used as inspiration to create and perform a range of movements that are put together to make an individual dance.

Teaching specific subject areas through a topic

While it is important to distinguish between the separate subject areas of history, design and technology and physical education, natural links can be difficult to ignore and are extremely useful in relating one area of work with another. One subject focus can provide opportunity to explore in another field.

A carefully planned topic can meld together prescribed areas of the curriculum to create interesting learning experiences appropriate to the needs of the class. Topic-based work presents a whole picture, motivates children and encourages their enthusiasm.

Getting started

Explore the accessibility of old toys for the children to see and possibly play with. Find out if a local museum has a collection of toys, examine how these are arranged and see if a guide will be available to talk to the children and answer their questions. There may be an arrangement whereby toys can be loaned to the school for a short time. Alternatively (or additionally), look into the possibility of a toy expert or enthusiast visiting the school to show and talk about a collection of relevant old toys.

Check the availability of the hall or other large floor space for the dance sessions. Decide on the arrangements and time required for the children to change their clothes before and after each dance activity, and for moving to and from the hall.

Make sure you are aware of any health problems and disabilities of individual children and consider how all of the children can become fully involved in each dance activity.

Involving parents and carers

Involving parents and carers is a useful strategy in helping to motivate children during their topic work on *Toys*. This topic is a particularly useful one, as most adults will be keen to share their own experiences of toys and childhood while, in turn, the children can share and compare information and new experiences with their parents.

At the beginning of the work on *Toys*, prepare a letter to parents and carers informing them of the areas of work in which their children will be involved. Explain why the children need to bring one of their own toys to school and that they need to practise their dance sequences. Point out how they can help by talking to their children about the toys that were special to them as children. Emphasise how important it is to listen as the children explain what they have discovered about toys and how their puppet is taking shape. As children progress with their dance ideas, parents can watch and encourage and help them remember their dance sequence.

Take this opportunity to ask parents and carers for the loan of books and toys relating to the

1950s, 60s and 70s, and earlier toys if they have any from their own parents. Where appropriate, ask for helpers to assist in the classroom as the children practise their sewing and joining techniques and move on to making their puppets. It may also be appropriate to ask for adults to accompany the class on a museum visit and request their help in videoing or photographing the children while they are practising and performing their dances.

Promise parents and carers that they will be able to visit the classroom to see the children's achievements relating to this topic, including an exhibition of the toys investigated. You may also want to organise 'public' performances by the puppets as well as the children's individual dances.

Introducing the topic to the children

Present the topic as an exciting one for both the children and yourself – something to look forward to, with interesting and progressive activities. Create a sense of fun and discovery. Tell them that they will be discovering more about toys; ones from the past as well as ones they are familiar with today. Explain that adults will be interested in hearing about the work in which the children are engaged, especially when looking at toys from the past. Parents and grandparents will enjoy sharing their memories about the toys they played with when they were children. Suggest to the children that they introduce the topic to their parents and carers. Encourage them to talk about what will be involved. About this time, inform parents by letter, explaining how they can help and contribute (see Involving parents, above).

Explain to the children that they are probably already experts themselves when talking about new toys and that people who know a lot about old toys will be able to help them find out about the past.

Inform the children that within their toys investigations, they will be looking closely at puppets and will be able to create a puppet for themselves. First, however, they will need to learn some new skills that will be needed in making them.

Explain that you are hoping that toys, and especially puppets, will give the children some good ideas for practising movements leading up to a special dance performance. This will mean they will be exercising their bodies in a purposeful and enjoyable way.

Starting points

It might be useful to elicit the children's initial responses on the subject of toys and possibly puppets. Find out which are the popular toys of the moment, those everyone wants and talks about. Do the children have any favourite toys they have kept since they were babies? Where do they keep their toys? Do they look after them and take care to tidy them away? Talk about inside and outside toys, toys to play with alone and those that are more fun if friends join in. Do the children know what their younger and/or older siblings like to play with? Perhaps ask the children what they think they might find out from a topic on toys.

Resources

During the dance sessions, have a video camera and a still camera (or a digital video camera) ready during sessions and look for opportunities to photograph the children as they work. Ideally, arrange for a parent or classroom assistant to take video film of the children as they work towards their finished performances. Cameras will also be useful during museum visits.

Try to collect or arrange as many as these other resources as possible:
■ a selection of modern toys that includes soft toys, games, models of vehicles, moving toys, construction kits, puzzles, toys that demonstrate new technology
■ a collection of old toys that could include dolls, teddy bears, train sets, model cars, jigsaw puzzles, other games and puzzles
■ books from the 50s, 60s and 70s that have pictures showing children playing with toys
■ museum services – any resources provided for children, guidebooks or pamphlets, photographs of displays
■ the services of an expert or enthusiast who can visit the class to talk about old toys
■ a collection of different types of puppets, including many different hand puppets, particularly some that will fit the children
■ video clips of puppet shows
■ art, craft and writing materials
■ different types of fabric – Binca, mesh, other open weave materials; non-fraying (such as felt), plain, furry and patterned materials
■ large-eyed needles, pins, thread, wool
■ buttons, sequins, braids, beads, other trimmings
■ plastic shapes and other templates
■ resealable bags
■ percussion instruments.

All kinds of toys

HISTORY

FOCUS
HISTORY
- describing an artefact
- communicating information about toys
- asking questions to find out more about the past
- characteristics of old and new objects
- similarities and differences between old and new toys
- sources that can be used to find out about the past

HISTORY

ACTIVITY 1

OUR FAVOURITE TOYS

© Ford Smith/Corbis

Learning objective
To describe an artefact and communicate information about it to others.

Resources
A selection of children's toys; paper; pencils and crayons.

Preparation
A few days before the activity, tell the children that you would like them to bring a favourite toy to school, and perhaps send a letter home to explain this request. Explain that the toy must not be too big, but something they can easily carry. Let them choose a toy from those in the classroom if they prefer. Remind the children the day before. Store the toys safely out of reach until required.

Activity
Arrange the toys in a group around which the children can sit in a large circle. Make some general comments about the toys: how exciting they look, how colourful they are, and how fortunate the children are to have such a selection to talk about.

Then ask the children how the toys could be sorted. If you think the children might need prompting, make comments that help to identify the range of toys: *I can see several soft toys, some games and a few models.* The children might suggest groups of dolls, games, toys with wheels, toys for playing with outdoors, toys for playing with a friend or by one's self, toys with moving parts. Decide upon satisfactory groupings. As there will probably not be enough time for each child to talk about their toy, ask the children to select a toy from each group and ask the owner to tell the class about this favourite toy. Ask questions if necessary: *How long have you had this toy? Do you remember where it came from? When do you play with it? Where do you keep it? Do you play with the toy by yourself or with other people? Can you say why it is your favourite toy?*

In pairs, the children can show each other their favourite toy, asking and answering appropriate questions.

Recording
Ask the children to draw the toy they have selected, labelling the important features and perhaps writing sentences to tell others why it is their favourite toy.

Differentiation
Children:
■ describe their favourite toy orally, draw it and label its parts
■ talk, draw, label and write about a favourite toy
■ ask and answer questions, draw, label and write a comprehensive description relating to a favourite toy.

Plenary
Point out how the children have exchanged information in different ways with each other about their toys, by asking and answering questions and by drawing and writing. Briefly introduce the idea of toys from the past by commenting that children all over the world have always enjoyed playing with toys and inventing games.

Display
As the children will want to take their toys home, display a small selection of classroom toys and trays into which they can be sorted. Provide labels to suggest criteria for sorting, such as *models*, *dolls*, *toys with wheels* and so on. Encourage the children to make up their own groupings too. Include the children's drawings and pieces of writing in the display.

ACTIVITY 2

OLD TOYS

HISTORY

Learning objectives
To use everyday words and phrases to describe an artefact; to understand that asking questions can help to find out about the past.

Resources
A range of toys (ideally about six to eight) from the past, such as an old doll or teddy bear, model car or other vehicle, a board game, construction kit, whip and top; books with pictures of children playing with toys such as their parents and grandparents might have had; a large box; a screen; photocopiable page 15; pencils and crayons.

Preparation
Conceal the selection of old toys in a large box. Arrange a screen, which could be a large piece of card folded into three, on a table.

**All kinds
of toys**

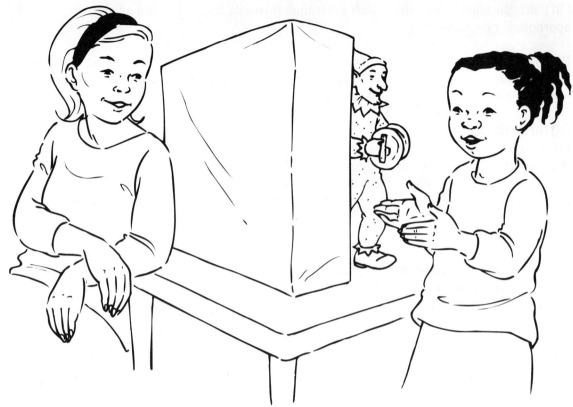

Activity

Begin by telling the children that you have some interesting toys for them to see. Explain that these toys are special because they are old. They were played with a long time ago, perhaps when their parents and grandparents were children.

Put the first toy on the table behind the screen and select a child to come up and to describe it to the rest of the class. Encourage the child to explain what they think the toy is, and then to talk about anything they think is interesting, perhaps its colour, its features, what it is made of and how it might be played with.

Invite the rest of the class to guess what the toy could be from information given in the description. Encourage them to ask the child describing the toy any questions that will help them to identify it.

Then remove the screen or display the toy for everyone to see. Ask the children to add to the description given so far and make further comments. Perhaps some of them have seen a similar toy that is new; perhaps a parent or grandparent has a toy like it at home. Suggest the children might like to find out more about the toy and encourage them to ask questions, for example: *Are there inside parts to see? How does the toy move? Does it make a noise? Is there a part of it missing? What does it say about it on the box? Does the toy still work properly?*

Repeat the process for the rest of the toys, choosing different children to describe each mystery artefact. Show some pictures of children playing with similar toys in the past to help the present-day children see how the toys were played with and build up an impression of childhood a long time ago.

Then ask the children to look at the old toys as a group. Do the children think they look old? What is it about them that makes them seem old? Who do they think would be able to tell them more about these toys? (Perhaps an adult who would have played with toys such as these when a child.)

Recording

Ask the children to choose one of the old toys to describe. Show them photocopiable page 15 and point out the spaces where they can draw the toy and describe it using labels, words and sentences. Then ask them to record anything they would like to know about the toy and what questions they could ask to find out more.

Differentiation

Children:
- help to describe an old toy orally, recording by drawing and writing words
- describe an old toy orally, suggest questions and record by drawing and writing sentences
- confidently describe an old toy orally, suggest relevant questions and record by drawing and sentences.

Plenary

Point out to the children that they are beginning to find out about the past by looking carefully at old toys. Explain that by asking questions they can find out even more. Consider who might be able to answer the questions. Suggest to the children that they talk to their parents/carers and grandparents about the toys they played with when they were children.

Display

Arrange the old toys for the children to see. Suggest that, as the toys are special, the children should just look at them, examining and playing with them only when given permission. Display the children's drawings of old toys along with the pictures in books.

ACTIVITY 3

HISTORY

TALKING ABOUT TOYS

Learning objective

To describe the characteristics of old and new objects.

Resources

A collection of old and new toys (carefully selected so that they are obviously old or obviously new), including a broken example among the new toys; photocopiable pages 16 and 17.

Preparation

Cut out the adjective word cards from photocopiable page 16 to describe toys. Have some spare cards on which to add other suitable adjectives the children suggest.

Activity

Put the toys in one large group around which the children can sit. Choose one of the old toys and ask the children to give you a word to describe the toy, to tell people that it is old. Perhaps the toy is rusty. Show the children the appropriate word card and place it next to the toy. Ask if there are any other toys that are rusty too. If so, put these together to make a group. Perhaps all the rusty toys are old? Can the children think of reasons why this is so? Suggest that new toys have not had time to become rusty; perhaps all the new toys are plastic and will not become rusty. Move on to use other adjectives, such as *faded* or *worn*, identifying, sorting and resorting, and discussing the toys. Talk about toys looking old because they have been played with a lot; how paper and card become dirty and torn, colours

© Image Club

All kinds of toys

fade. Toys made from fabric can fray, develop holes and become unstitched. Parts of toys get lost. Point out, however, that new toys can get broken too if not cared for. Show the children a new toy that has been broken.

Talk about the fact that these old toys have survived and were not lost or thrown away. Encourage the children to imagine the adventures the toys have had, where they were kept, the games they were involved in, different owners they might have had and so on. If necessary to provide inspiration, describe some adventures a particular toy might have had, starting when it was newly made, if it was given as a birthday or Christmas present, who it belonged to, how it was used, if it travelled and where it has been since its owner grew up.

Recording

Ask the children to make up an adventure for one of the old toys. This could be recorded in the storyboards on photocopiable page 17 as a sequence of pictures with titles or sentences and arrows linking each stage. Provide only three boxes for the children, if more appropriate, by covering up two of the boxes before you photocopy the page.

© Bettmann/Corbis

Differentiation

Children:
■ recognise differences between old and new toys and with help draw a simple sequence of events in the life of an old toy
■ recognise differences between old and new toys and devise a sequence of events in the life of an old toy, using drawings and headings
■ recognise old and new toys and devise an imaginative sequence of events in the life of an old toy using drawings, headings and sentences.

Plenary

Look at some of the toys' adventures. Have the toys always had a happy life? Did any have a narrow escape and are lucky still to be around? Ask the children what happens to their toys these days when they have finished with them. Do they give them away so that they can go on having further adventures until the time when they will be called old? Do the children have any toys they will still keep when they are grown up?

Display

Arrange the storyboards where the children can look at each other's ideas and explain their own work.

HISTORY

ACTIVITY 4

THEN AND NOW

Learning objective

To recognise similarities and differences between old and new toys.

Resources

Pairs of obviously old and new toys, such as teddy bears, trains, jigsaws, dolls, model cars (a metal toy car to compare with a plastic toy car of a current make and model; the new jigsaw should have an up-to-date scene or character or unusual shape; the old one might show children playing in the 50s, 60s or 70s); photocopiable page 18; paper; pencils and crayons.

Activity

Choose an old and a new example of the same type of toy, perhaps two teddy bears. Ask the children which they think is the old bear and which the new. Was it easy for them to tell? Encourage the children to tell you which clues helped them to decide. Perhaps the new bear is very clean, brightly coloured and has no signs of wear. The old bear may have been well looked after but somehow seems less new. Perhaps its fur has faded and its eyes are less bright. The fabrics of which the bears are made can also give clues.

Look at other examples. Can the children identify the old and the new and give good reasons for their decisions? Old toy trains and cars will be made of different materials, and the new ones will probably be modern designs representing real cars and trains currently in use. An old jigsaw will have an old-fashioned picture, a new one might show a scene from space or recently invented characters. Explain that the word *modern* applies to items made in the present or very recent times.

Recording

Ask the children to choose two of the same type of toy, an old example and a new example. They should draw each toy and use labels to indicate the similarities and differences. Alternatively, provide photocopiable page 18 on which there are pictures of old and new toys that can be compared by labelling and writing relevant sentences.

Differentiation

Children:
■ recognise some differences between similar old and new toys
■ compare old and new toys, pointing out the differences with drawings and labels
■ compare old and new toys, indicating differences in drawings and explanatory sentences.

Plenary

Talk about toys looking modern or old-fashioned, that new toys and new characters are always being invented and that a broken toy is not necessarily an old toy.

Display

Arrange old and new versions of similar toys together with the children's work.

ACTIVITY 5

FINDING OUT ABOUT THE PAST

HISTORY

Learning objective

To appreciate that oral sources can be used to find out about the past.

Resources

A visitor to school who can talk from personal experience and present a collection of old toys; a still camera; a video camera; paper; pencils and crayons.

Preparation

Talk to the visitor beforehand and explain exactly what you would like him or her to tell the children. The speaker could be an expert in old toys or a local person able to share her childhood experiences. She will need to show and demonstrate some of the toys in her collection and talk about how she enjoyed playing with them during her childhood. Provide a surface on which the artefacts can be displayed. Explain that you would like the children to ask questions, so create suitable opportunities and even ask the children to practise asking some generic questions that may be appropriate. Consider that some aspects could be left unexplained; and you could suggest the visitor retires for refreshments while questions are discussed, returning to answer them during a second session.

Activity

Prepare the children for the visit of the toy enthusiast. Tell them that older people will have played with toys when they were children and these toys will have been different from the ones the children are familiar with today. Explain that a good way of finding out about the past is to talk to people who have had experiences of what they are researching or wanting to find out about and to ask them questions. (Refer to 'Old toys' on page 9 if appropriate, and remind the children of how asking questions was useful in finding out about the toys then.) People often save artefacts such as toys, and children today can look at these to find out what life was like before they were born.

Arrange the children where they can easily see the speaker and the toys, and can sit comfortably. Introduce the visitor and ask the children to listen carefully to find out more about the past. They will be able to ask questions afterwards. Help to guide the question session, encouraging quieter children to contribute to the discussion. If necessary, suggest questions the children can ask, but encourage spontaneity. Tell the children they should continue to listen carefully to avoid asking questions that have already been answered. Ask the visitor's permission to take photographs and/or video footage during the presentation and of the display of toys.

Afterwards, thank the speaker and explain how much everyone has learned about toys and how they were played with in the past.

Recording

Ask the children to write a personal account describing their impressions of the visitor and the toys. They should record some of the things they have found out and perhaps draw and describe a toy they were particularly interested in.

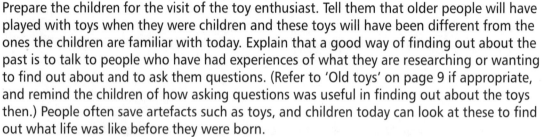

Differentiation

Children:
■ are aware that they can find out about the past by listening to people and asking questions
■ know that oral sources can provide useful information about the past, writing a simple account indicating what they have found out
■ understand that oral sources can be an important way of finding out about the past, writing a detailed account of what they have found out.

Plenary

Talk about how much has been discovered from the visit by the toy expert. Comment on how useful it was to be able to ask questions of someone who had played with the toys. Emphasise that this is a good method of finding out about the past.

Display

Write captions for the photographs you have taken and arrange them together with the children's accounts of the visit.

Old toys

Draw and write about one of the old toys you have looked at.

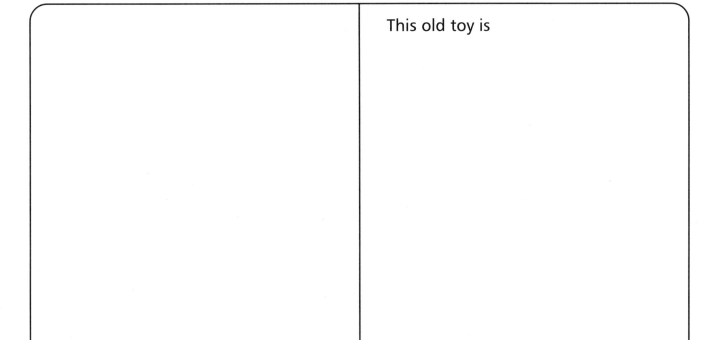

This old toy is

What I would like to know

Questions I would like to ask

Toys word cards

rusty	bright
broken	worn
faded	scratched
shiny	modern
dull	old-fashioned

Talking about toys

Imagine an adventure the old toy might have had.

1.

2.

3.

4.

5.

SCHOLASTIC

Toys then and now

Compare these pairs of toys.

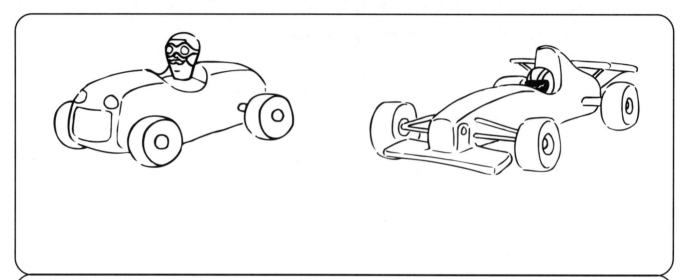

Puppets

Section 2

FOCUS

DESIGN & TECHNOLOGY
■ different types of puppets and their purpose
■ puppets are made up of different parts
■ how puppets can be used
■ making simple drawings and labelling parts

DESIGN & TECHNOLOGY

PE
■ exploring movement ideas

PE

ACTIVITY 1

DIFFERENT PUPPETS

DESIGN & TECHNOLOGY

Learning objectives
To know about the purpose of puppets and that there are different types.

Resources
A collection of different types of puppets, especially hand and finger puppets; paper; pencils and crayons.

Preparation
A few days before the activity, ask the children to bring to school puppets of any type that they have.

Activity
Present the children with a selection of puppets. Perhaps not all children are familiar with this type of toy. Encourage the children to tell you what they think a puppet is. They might talk about a puppet being a special kind of toy, one which has a particular character, can be given a voice and is designed to be made to move and act by the person controlling it. Decide what you might call the person in charge of a puppet's actions. This could be the puppet master, puppet operator or puppeteer. Point out that the character of a puppet can be manipulated in whatever way the puppet master decides.

Look at some individual puppets and discuss them with the children. Choose a very simple example first, such as a hand or finger puppet, and demonstrate how to bring it to life with a few movements and perhaps a voice or other sound. Ask the children how you are making the puppet move and talk. They should tell you that your fingers and perhaps thumb, as well as your voice, are being used to work the puppet and make it seem alive. Look at other puppets that are made in a more complicated way. Discuss what it is that makes these work, for example a rod or strings. Perhaps one has an in-built squeak or other noise. Relate the way the puppets have been made to the method by which they are operated and the flexibility of their movements.

Move on to discuss the appearance and characters of the puppets. Can the children recognise any characters, perhaps models of a television puppet? What other figures are among the collection? There could be pirates, princesses, astronauts, famous characters from stories the children know. Perhaps some are animals. Group the puppets by appearance, for example friendly, frightening, happy, sad.

Look briefly at the parts of the puppets. They will all have a head. Notice whether it is a separate part or is continuous with the body. Identify any arms, legs, tails, flippers and so on.

In groups, give the children the opportunity to handle a favourite puppet and talk to each other about it.

Recording
Ask the children to write about one of the puppets they have discussed, describing what they like about it. Encourage them to add a drawing and to explain what they think its character is like and what it is about the puppet that tells them this. Some children can compare two different puppets, describing their similarities and differences.

Differentiation
Children:
■ are aware that there are toys called puppets and there are different types; make a drawing of a puppet
■ are aware of different types of puppets that can be manipulated to represent characters; write a description of a puppet and its character
■ are aware of different types of puppets that can be manipulated to represent characters; describe similarities and differences between puppets.

Plenary
Remind the children that they have examined all sorts of puppets and talk about how they can be different from ordinary toys. Emphasise that the puppet's character can be manipulated by the person who controls its actions.

Display
Arrange the puppets so the children can observe their differences. Have a small selection of puppets available to be handled. Display the children's explanations and illustrations with the puppets.

ACTIVITY 2

PARTS OF PUPPETS

DESIGN & TECHNOLOGY

Learning objectives
To know that puppets are made up of different parts; to make simple drawings and label parts.

Resources
A collection of hand and finger puppets, including characters from different cultures; photocopiable pages 23–5; pencils and crayons.

Preparation
Add words to the word cards on photocopiable pages 23 and 24 if appropriate, then copy, cut and laminate the word cards, making enough sets for each child or pair of children.

Activity
Present the children with a selection of hand and finger puppets. If there are enough, pairs of children could share a puppet to examine and ask and answer questions about, as the discussion proceeds. Look at the puppets closely. Can the children identify arms, a head and parts of the face? Do some have legs? Are the bodies made from separate parts or are they all

in one? Some might have a head that is a separate part, in others it might be a simpler extension of the body.

It might be appropriate to refer to the word cards during the discussion, otherwise go through them with the children prior to recording.

Next, ask the children what the puppets are made of. You could sort them into groups: *This puppet is made of felt. Is there another made of similar fabric?* Ask which children have puppets made of fluffy fabric.

Establish how the parts of the puppets are fastened together. Are there puppets with parts that are glued or sewed together? Is it easy to tell how the parts are joined? Can any stitches be seen? Explain the use of the word *seam* and refer to the word cards during this discussion.

Talk about the parts that give the puppets their distinguishing characters. What has been added to make each puppet different? Perhaps there are patterns and features sewn on the basic shape or extra pieces of fabric to create ears, wings and so on. Beads and other decorations may have been glued on. Does their puppet have hair, a hat, other clothes?

Draw attention to the opening where a hand or finger is inserted to operate the puppet. Discuss the size and position of the opening. Has any special sewing or gluing been necessary to make this part?

Finally, ask the children if they think their puppet is well made, and who they think it was made for.

Recording
Ask the children to describe a puppet they have examined. Provide them with photocopiable page 25 and encourage them to make a detailed diagram. Suggest to the children that they label as many parts of the puppet as they can and make notes in the small boxes to add to the description. Remind them to refer to the word cards for help.

Differentiation
Children:
■ make a simple drawing of a hand or finger puppet and label the parts
■ draw a hand or finger puppet, describing the different parts with accurate labels and adding simple notes on its construction
■ make a detailed, labelled drawing of a hand or finger puppet with relevant notes relating to its construction.

Plenary
Remind the children of the different puppets they have examined. Point out that some are very simple in their design and others have more detailed features. Comment particularly on any different designs for the way the heads or arms were made.

Display
Use the children's diagrams and notes to add to the display, with the word cards.

ACTIVITY 3

PUPPETS COME TO LIFE

DESIGN & TECHNOLOGY   PE

Learning objectives
To be aware of how puppets can be used; to explore movement ideas.

Resources
Video footage of one or two puppet sequences; pictures of other puppet characters the children might know; paper; pencils and crayons.

2

Puppets

Preparation
Locate some video film of puppet shows. Ideally find footage with the puppets 'acting' a story theme and a second sequence that delivers a message, such as road safety or recycling information.

Activity
Talk about puppets coming to life and performing when someone decides to play with them, and show some of the puppet pictures. Point out that although puppets often have their own characters, which we can tell from their designs, what they do, how they move and what they say depends on the person who is operating them. Go on to explain that two or more puppets can perform together to create a scene or a story.

Show the children a short video film of puppets performing a story. If necessary, tell them beforehand the names of the characters involved. Afterwards, ask the children to recall the storyline. Encourage the children to discuss the characters, describing each one and linking the appearance of each puppet with its actions. What was it that made a character scary, funny or sad? Did the appearance of the puppet fit with its actions? How did the movements and body positions of the puppets help in the telling of the story? Use appropriate vocabulary, such as *jump, bounce, spin, turn, freeze, statue*. Talk about direction – *forwards*, *backwards*, *sideways*; and space – *near*, *far*, *on the spot*, *alone*.

Show the film again so that the children can relate points of the discussion to the performance. Ask them to take a special look at the expressions on the faces of the puppets as well as their movements and think about how these features represent their characters.

Show the children a second short film, one intended to deliver a message. Ask the children to look out for any differences in this puppet show. They might comment on the range of characters, expressions and movements, and the way the puppets perform. Make sure the children understand the message that the puppets present. Do they think the puppets did a good job? Did the children enjoy the performance?

Recording
The children can describe the story or the message of one of the puppet shows with sentences and drawings. Encourage them to describe the puppets, explaining how their appearance and characteristics were linked. Ask them to mention which puppet characters they liked and any they disliked.

© 2003/Rolf Richardson/Alamy.com

Differentiation
Children:
■ are aware of how puppets can be used for performances; can recognise different movements
■ describe how different puppets represent different characters in performances; recognise and describe different movements
■ describe and compare puppet characters in different situations, giving opinions on their performances; accurately describe a range of movements.

Plenary
Ask the children to recall what they enjoyed about the puppet performances and what they have learned from them. Talk about how puppets are used to represent characters to amuse us, frighten us, make us laugh, teach us and help us to remember things (refer to the message of the video film).

Display
Arrange the pictures of puppet characters together with the children's work.

Puppet word cards (1)

hand	eye
mouth	nose
ear	face
body	head
arm	

Puppet word cards (2)

seam	beads
thread	wool
fur	glue
sew	stitches
fabric	

Parts of puppets

Draw a puppet and label the parts.

What is the puppet made of?

How is it fastened together?

What details have been added?

Displaying toys

FOCUS

HISTORY
- talking about objects from the past
- sorting toys according to different criteria
- sequencing objects in time
- displaying toys to communicate what has been learned
- the organisation of museum exhibits

HISTORY

ACTIVITY 1

OLD AND NEW – APPEARANCE

Learning objectives
To decide whether an object is old or new; to describe the characteristics of toys relating to appearance and style.

Resources
A collection of old and new toys; books showing pictures of old toys; the word cards from photocopiable page 16; paper; pencils and crayons.

Preparation
Carefully choose toys which can easily be identified as old or new by their appearance. Select bright, modern toys to contrast with worn, faded examples of old toys. Try to include old toys with obviously dated styles and presentation. Avoid modern toys made in an old-fashioned style or representing obsolete objects, such as a plastic steam train.

Activity
Show the children the collection of toys. Encourage them to make comments and share their first impressions. They should recognise that some of the toys are old and some are new. Show the children the word cards and suggest sorting the toys into two groups – old and new. Choose children in turn to identify a toy and tell the class which group they think it belongs to. When the sorting is complete, encourage the children to focus on the appearance of the toys. Ask them to look at one group and then the other and tell you what differences they see. Perhaps the group of new toys looks brighter and more colourful. Ask the children why they think this should be so. They might suggest the old toys have faded through use and age and so look duller than the new toys. The paint on the old toys might be scratched and worn, or there are signs of rust while the new toys are still shiny. Comment on the toys made from soft fabrics – the older ones might be paler, have holes and seams and edges that are beginning to fray. Other toys might have some paper parts that have torn.

Next, compare the designs and styles of the toys. What are the children's feelings about the old toys? Do they find the characters, written material or patterns strange and unfamiliar? Can they recognise the features and designs of the new toys more easily? Talk about old-fashioned and modern objects. Remind the children that *old-fashioned* relates to things from the past that perhaps their parents/carers or grandparents used as children, and *modern* means everything we find new today. Show the children pictures of children playing with old toys.

Recording
Ask the children to choose one old toy and one new toy to draw and describe. Suggest they label their pictures to show how they can tell the toy is old or new and add notes or sentences for further explanation. Remind the children to use the appearance adjectives on the word cards in their descriptions.

Differentiation
Children:
■ distinguish between old and new toys, showing differences in appearance in labelled drawings
■ distinguish between old and new toys, using labelled drawings and sentences to make comparisons of appearance
■ distinguish between old and new toys, using drawings, labels and sentences to make comparisons of appearance, style and design.

Plenary
Talk about distinguishing old toys from new, asking the children to tell each other how they might decide by just looking at them.

Display
Arrange the two groups of toys with their labels. Add labels with adjectives relating to individual toys in each group. Display the children's labelled drawings near by.

HISTORY

ACTIVITY 2

OLD AND NEW – MATERIALS AND MOVEMENT

Learning objective
To describe characteristics of old and new objects, referring to materials and movement.

Resources
Groups of old and new toys; photocopiable page 35; pencils and crayons.

Preparation
Ensure that among the toys selected for this activity there are examples of different materials such as wood, metal, plastic, paper and fabric, and with quite obvious differences between the old and the new. Other examples should contrast aspects of technology, particularly means of movement. Include new toys that are powered by batteries or solar panels, for example, to compare with old toys that use clockwork or other simple mechanisms.

Activity
Arrange the two groups of toys for the children to see. Ask if they can tell how you have sorted the toys. From previous activities they should recognise a group of old toys and a group of new ones. Explain that this time you will be looking for special differences between the groups. First ask the children to tell each other what they notice about the materials of

3

Displaying
toys

which the toys in each group are made. Talk about the old toys made of wood and metal and compare them with the plastic toys of the new group. Examine the fabric toys of each group. Are there any noticeable differences between the old-fashioned fabrics and modern ones? Similarly, are there comparisons to be made between any toys made with paper or cardboard? Make generalisations: *More of the old toys are made of wood. There are no metal toys among the new toys. Lots of new toys are made of plastic. New fabrics are more brightly coloured than old fabrics.*

  Move on to discuss how the toys move and are operated. Examine the old toys and encourage the children to try out the mechanisms and give their comments. How effective is a clockwork toy? Why is a pull-along toy suitable for a baby? Then talk about the new toys and their operations. Which toys are powered by a battery? …a solar panel? …a computer? Explain that these are quite new inventions and would not have been available for children a long time ago. Find out which is the children's favourite moving old toy and which new toy's movement they find most interesting.

Recording
Show the children photocopiable page 35. Explain that the instructions ask them to draw two different toys, an old wooden toy and a modern plastic toy, and to identify the two illustrations. Ask them to give their drawings titles and to write a sentence explaining how the moving toys are operated. Advise them to use the vocabulary list given at the bottom of the sheet.

Differentiation
Children:
■ recognise the characteristics of new and old toys relating to materials and movement and record this using drawings
■ describe and compare the characteristics of old and new toys relating to materials and movement, recording this with drawings and sentences
■ discuss and compare the characteristics of old and new toys relating to materials and movement, showing their understanding of the differences when recording.

Plenary
Explain to the children that all sorts of new materials have been developed and new techniques for making and powering things have been discovered since their parents and grandparents were children. This means that new toys have been invented that are quite different from those of the past. Children in the future will probably have very different toys to play with.

Display
Use labels to indicate the differences in materials and movement of old and new toys and exhibit these near to the children's recording.

HISTORY

ACTIVITY 3

VISITING A MUSEUM

Learning objective
To understand that museum displays can be used to find out about the past.

Resources
Access to a local toy museum and its resources; clipboards; paper; pencils and crayons; a still camera; a video camera.

Preparation

Arrange for the children to visit a toy museum. Find out what is available and take advantage of any assistance, such as resource packs, hands-on activities and experts to talk to the children. Prepare the children for the visit, arrange adult helpers and check LEA and school guidelines for out-of-school visits.

Activity

Tell the children that they will be visiting a museum. Explain that things used in the past are often saved by people and specially displayed for people today to see. Find out if any of the children have previously visited a museum and can explain to the others what it was like. Point out that the museum they will be visiting has displays of old toys that were played with a long time ago. From these they will be able to find out about children's play in the past. Let the children know that they will be able to take part in activities and ask questions.

On the day of the visit, make sure the children are completely familiar with the arrangements at the museum and know which friends they will be with and the adult who will be looking after them. Inform them of any talks, activities and tasks they will be expected to do.

Encourage the children to listen carefully to anyone explaining things to them, to ask questions at appropriate times, to look carefully at the exhibits and to make careful drawings of interesting toys when asked. Point out how the artefacts are displayed. Take photographs where allowed and video footage for reference back in the classroom. Ensure the children appreciate the time given by the museum staff, thanking them before they leave.

Recording

At the museum, the children can draw and make notes about the most interesting toys and displays. Back in the classroom, ask them to recall what they enjoyed about their visit. Play the video if you made one. They can record what they have found out about children's lives in the past and what they noticed about how the exhibits were displayed. This could take the form of a letter to the museum staff thanking them for their help during the visit. Make photocopies of any letters that are sent.

Differentiation

Children:
■ are aware that a museum display offers opportunities to find out about the past
■ are aware that a museum display provides a range of useful information which can tell them about the past
■ understand the importance of a museum display in finding out about the past.

Plenary

Ask the children why they think you arranged the visit to the toy museum for them. Make sure they understand that looking at artefacts collected together in a museum helps them to find out about the past. Asking questions to discover more about the exhibits also helps them to build up a picture of what life was like before they were born.

Display

Mount the children's accounts or copies of the letters as well as any photographs taken at the museum. Add captions and explanations.

Displaying toys

HISTORY

ACTIVITY 4

SORTING OLD TOYS

Learning objectives
To sort objects in different ways; to understand how museum exhibits are organised.

Resources
A collection of old toys that can be sorted into groups such as the materials of which they are made, their movement, who might play with them and so on; video film from the previous activity (or see Preparation, below); photocopiable page 36; paper; pencils and crayons; scissors; glue.

Preparation
Children will need to be familiar with the way objects from the past are displayed in a museum. Refer to the previous activity and if a visit to a suitable local museum has not been possible, use video footage or pictures from the Internet to introduce children to the idea of displaying items for others to see. Perhaps invite a collector of childhood memorabilia to visit and provide a temporary display. (See also 'Finding out about the past' on page 13 in section 1.)

Activity
Talk about possessing a collection of old or unusual objects and wanting to show them to other people. Point out the classroom collection of toys from the past. Explain that it would be a good idea to put them on display for people to see. Encourage the children to think about how this could this be achieved. They might suggest showing and talking about individual items, especially if a visitor has demonstrated this in the classroom. Move on to talk about displaying the items for people to look at for themselves, as in a museum. Talk about how the items need to be organised and arranged in an appealing and informative way, not randomly or in a jumble.

Show the toys you have available. Have the children any ideas for the display arrangement? Listen to all suggestions. Focus on some of the ideas and ask the children to help with the sorting. Perhaps the toys could be sorted according to the materials of which they are made: wooden toys, metal toys, toys made of soft fabric. Depending on the range of toys available, other groups could include toys for babies and children of different ages, toys that are games, toys with wheels, toys to play outside with and so on. Things that do not fit into an obvious group can be temporarily put aside.

Either leave the toys arranged in suitable groups that might help the children with their recording, or present them as a random collection so the children can choose their own method of sorting.

Recording
Ask the children to record a method they like for sorting the toys available. Show them how, using a suitable template, they can use large circles or oval shapes in which to draw and label groups of toys. Alternatively, provide the children with photocopiable page 36 which shows a

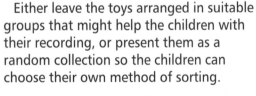

range of toys that they can sort. Tell the children to cut out the pictures and stick them into labelled groups. Some children might be able to use a Venn diagram to demonstrate that some toys fit into more than one group. They can put the pictures on photocopiable page 36 in the correct sections of the diagram.

Differentiation
Children:
■ sort toys according to suggested criteria, recording the groups as drawings
■ suggest criteria for grouping toys, recording this using diagrams
■ suggest several criteria for grouping toys, recording ideas as diagrams, including a Venn diagram.

Plenary
Remind the children that there are different ways of grouping items such as toys, especially if they are to be presented as in a museum. Look at some of the ways the children have recorded. What do they think can be learned from their displays? Has anyone found a very different or unusual way of sorting the toys?

Display
In pairs or groups, give the children the opportunity to arrange the toys as a display, providing labels to indicate the groups. Shallow boxes or PE hoops can be used to contain the toys. Add the children's ideas for grouping toys.

ACTIVITY 5

SEQUENCING TOYS IN TIME

HISTORY

Learning objectives
To talk about everyday objects in the past; to sequence objects in time.

Resources
A selection of toys – some old and some modern; photocopiable page 37; card; pencils and crayons.

Preparation
Find a suitable area in the classroom where space is available to arrange toys as on a timeline. This could be a long working surface with a display board behind. Choose three toys for the initial sequencing – one that is very old, one less old and one that is very new.

Activity
Talk to the children a little more about setting up a museum-style display of the collection of old toys. Remind the children of the purpose of a museum display, that it allows people to see interesting items and perhaps learn more about them. Refer to the reason for sorting the toys in the previous activity: so that people can see groups of similar objects easily.

© Image Club

3

Displaying toys

Explain that it is also useful to sort things according to how old they are, and that exhibits can be arranged in a line starting with the oldest and ending with the newest.

Show the children three toys from different periods. The children will easily recognise the newest toy. It will be bright and colourful with an up-to-date design and mechanism. It is probably one they all know well because similar toys are in the shops now and lots of people have them.

Next, ask for suggestions as to which is the oldest. Remind the children of previous activities where they have looked at toys from the past. Help the children to decide why they think this toy is the oldest. Perhaps it appears dull, it is very worn, the design seems old-fashioned and it moves using an outdated mechanism.

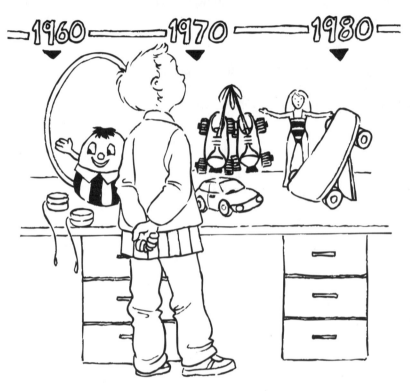

Point out that, since the children have identified the oldest and newest toys, the remaining toy must be in the middle. Talk briefly about its appearance and design in comparison with the other two toys.

Consider who will have played with the older toys. Suggest that the oldest toy might have been played with by the children's grandparents when they were children and the next oldest toy by their parents. The children themselves would play with the newest toy.

Arrange these three toys on the display area where a timeline can be developed. Choose other toys from the collection and ask the children for their ideas on where they can be fitted in. Help the children to decide by talking about who would have played with the toys – parents, grandparents or the children themselves.

Recording

Show the children photocopiable page 37, which presents groups of toys on a timeline. Identify the toys illustrated and ask who would play with each of them. Ask the children to draw a third group of toys in the blank box, to represent those they might play with themselves. They could draw a modern car, doll and hand-held computer game, for example. Underneath the pictures they can label them with who would have played with the toys – grandparents, parents, themselves.

Differentiation

Children:
■ complete a simple sequence of toys in time
■ know that some toys are older than others and complete a simple sequence in time
■ can sort toys according to age and complete a simple sequence in time.

Plenary

Explain that a useful way of showing and sorting toys in a museum is to put them in order of how old they are, starting with the oldest and working towards the newest. Point out that this is known as a timeline sequence.

Display

To complete the timeline display, use the children's labels either fastened to the board behind the timeline or as free-standing folded cards.

ACTIVITY 6

HISTORY

A TOY MUSEUM

Learning objective
To communicate in a variety of ways what has been learned about toys.

Resources
A collection of old and new toys; paper; card; pencils and crayons.

Preparation
Decide upon details for a toy museum, such as its position in the classroom, the amount of space available and how previous displays and arrangements can be incorporated.

Activity
Ask the children who might like to see the collection of toys. They might suggest older people; especially parents and grandparents who might have played with some of the toys during their childhood and would be very pleased to be reminded of those days. Other children would like to find out about the toys too, as children are always interested in things they can play with.

Point out that before anyone visits, the exhibits must be properly arranged with suitable labels and information provided so that everyone will know what they are looking at. Refer to the groups into which the children have sorted the toys and the timeline that helps people to compare the ages of toys. Remind the children of any museums they have visited and talk about how the exhibits were arranged.

Ask the children for ideas about how people will use their toy museum. From this discussion, decide how information about toys will be passed on to others. Suggest giving guided tours. Point out that guides need to know all about the exhibits so that they can explain to visitors what the toys are and why they have been arranged in such a way. Take on the role of a museum guide and demonstrate an individual item or group of toys. Ask some children to do the same, allowing them to choose an area of the collection in which they are particularly knowledgeable and interested.

Discuss the possibility of making a guidebook that visitors could use while looking around if there is no one available to act as a guide (see Activity 7, below). Finally, make sure the children understand that the displayed items need labelling with short pieces of information as necessary.

Listen to any other ideas the children have about developing their museum, such as creating a box office where tickets are issued and providing a visitors' book for comments.

Recording
Use the children's work to create a programme for the museum. Allocate sections of the exhibits for groups, pairs or individuals to concentrate on. Perhaps decide on a format so that the children follow the same plan when providing information. Collect together the children's work and if possible laminate the pages if there is to be only one copy. Children can design and print out invitations using appropriate computer software.

Differentiation
Children:
■ speak and write about the museum display to pass on what they have found out
■ are aware of different ways of communicating and can speak and write about the museum exhibits
■ understand the purpose of a museum and can communicate information about exhibits by speaking and writing.

3

Displaying
toys

Plenary
Talk about the success of the toy museum, how splendid the displays look and how interested visitors will be. Emphasise the importance of sorting the toys and providing information.

Display
Develop the museum in a special area of the classroom by creating displays using the children's work. Provide an entrance with ticket office, attendant and information about opening times. Offer a guide book and guides.

HISTORY

ACTIVITY 7

PREPARING A GUIDEBOOK

Learning objective
To communicate what has been learned about toys

Resources
Collection of old toys; paper; a ring binder or similar; pencils and crayons.

Preparation
Decide which items from the toy museum exhibition will be most useful for the children to describe. Alternatively, each child could choose a toy to describe.

Activity
Discuss the operation of the museum which the children have set up. Talk about how visitors to the museum need information about the exhibits. Relate the facilities of the museum the children visited with those of the class museum.

Suggest the class works together to compile a special guide book for the museum. Explain that each person prepares one page of the guidebook with all the pages put together to create a whole book. Ask the children what they think should be included on each page. They might suggest the name of the toy, a drawing and description, perhaps how it works and any instructions required about how to play with the toy.

Recording
Let the children make their pages. Point out where the heading could be written and the box for the drawing.

Differentiation
Children:
■ draw and describe a toy to contribute information to a guidebook
■ communicate what has been learned about a toy by creating a page for a guidebook
■ understand the importance of communicating what has been found out about a toy by providing information for a guidebook.

Plenary
Ask the children who will find the guidebook useful. Suggest they observe how visitors use the book and perhaps ask them what they have learned. Emphasise the importance of the children's work in providing information for others to see.

Display
Provide a suitable cover for the book. With the children's help, prepare an index and draw visitors' attention to the children's work.

Old and new – materials and movement

Draw an old wooden toy.

Draw a new plastic toy.

Describe the old moving toy and the new moving toy.

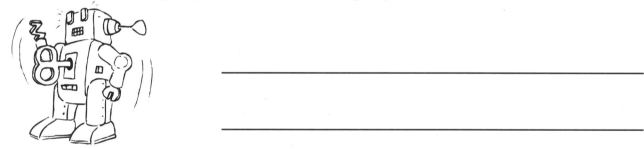

_____

_____

_____

_____

batteries   movement   metal   wind-up

clockwork   wood   material   plastic   design

Sorting old toys

A timeline of toys

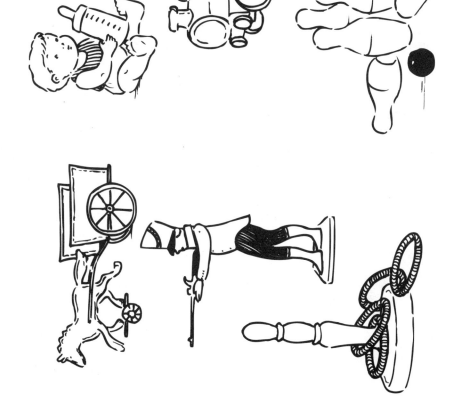

modern

old

very old

SCHOLASTIC

Section 4

New techniques

DESIGN & TECHNOLOGY

FOCUS

DESIGN & TECHNOLOGY
■ practising techniques prior to making a puppet
■ practising simple sewing techniques
■ using a template
■ joining materials

DESIGN & TECHNOLOGY

ACTIVITY 1

BASIC SEWING

Learning objective
To practise basic sewing techniques.

Resources
Small pieces of open-weave fabric, such as types of mesh, hessian, Binca and so on; plain fabric; large-eyed needles; lengths of fine wool and thick sewing thread; scissors; thin card or strong paper for mounting children's work; pencils.

Preparation
Decide how the sewing session will be organised. Ideally the children should be together for the introductory part of the activity, working in groups later, with an adult to supervise. Attach a threaded needle to pieces of open-weave material for each child's first effort.

Activity
Explain to the children that it is very useful to be able to make simple stitches with a needle and thread. Ask if they have any ideas as to when sewing might be useful. They might suggest making or mending clothes, fastening pieces of fabric together, attaching buttons to garments, creating patterns on fabric with different stitches. Find out whether they have seen any adults using a needle and thread for sewing or embroidery. Perhaps some of the children have practised sewing already and are willing to share their experiences.

Tell the children that they will be able to try sewing for themselves. Show them a piece of open-weave fabric and a needle. Explain how the needle has a hole called an 'eye' at one end and a sharp point at the other. Briefly emphasise the importance of using a needle safely and sensibly. Show how the thread is passed through the eye of the needle – 'threading the needle' ready for sewing.

Then demonstrate running stitches on a piece of open-weave fabric. Point out to the children that the holes make it easy to push the needle through the fabric as well as helping to keep the stitches in a straight line.

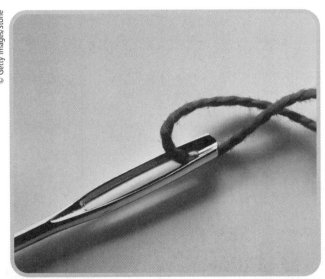

© Getty images/Stone

Give the children the opportunity to try running stitches for themselves, using a small piece of fabric onto which a needle with thread has been attached. Encourage them to work in a straight line and to keep the stitches even by counting the holes in the fabric.

Next, show the children how to attach a piece of thread to the fabric by making two or three stitches on top of each other. Explain that this firmly fastens the thread to the fabric before they begin. Let the children practise more running stitches, this time starting off by themselves.

Finally explain that when the thread has almost been used, it is important to finish off carefully. Show how overlapping stitches can make a firm ending as well as a beginning. Point out that enough thread must be left to carry out the finishing-off process. Suggest the children watch each other as they work to help them remember what to do.

Children who have successfully reached this stage can try sewing on different materials and with different types of threads.

Differentiation
Children:
■ use a needle and thread to make running stitches
■ use a needle and thread to make running stitches, joining the thread to the fabric and finishing off
■ handle a needle and thread confidently to make running stitches on different fabrics, starting and finishing off successfully.

Plenary
Encourage the children to show each other their efforts. Admire straight lines and even stitches. Ask the children to check their starting and finishing off. Is the thread firmly attached and will the stitches stay in place? Will they remember how to start and finish the next time they sew?

Display
Staple children's work to thin card or strong paper. Encourage them to add a title and their name: 'My sewing by Kim', 'Running stitches by Dilip'.

ACTIVITY 2

USING A TEMPLATE

DESIGN & TECHNOLOGY

Learning objective
To use a template to mark out identical shapes.

Resources
Plastic shapes and other items that can be used as templates; pieces of non-stretchy, easy-to-cut fabric, plain and patterned; scissors; thin card; pencils; rulers; stapler; glue; mounting paper.

Preparation
Decide how the session will be organised. After the introduction and demonstration, children can work in groups with an adult as supervisor.

Activity
Point out that an easy way of making shapes is to draw around something that is already the size and shape you need. Refer to other activities where the children may have created shapes by using templates. Perhaps they have made pictures in this way or have made shapes in which to write, collect words and so on. Demonstrate drawing around a plastic square on a

4

New techniques

piece of paper. Point out how this must be done slowly and carefully on a flat surface. Then cut out the shape and compare the new shape with the original. Explain that a shape that is useful for making other shapes is called a 'template'. Use the square template to make a second outline and point out that many outlines can be made and they will all be exactly the same.

Then explain that shapes can also be made from fabric in the same way. Show the children how to use the template on a piece of plain cloth and cut this out. Tell the children that cutting cloth is not usually as easy as cutting paper, but again identical squares are made.

Suggest the children practise making their own shapes. Provide simple instructions. For example: *Make two identical rectangles out of blue paper. Cut two triangles out of green fabric.* Children can move on to shapes with curves after they have practised straight-line shapes: *Make three circles out of a bright-coloured fabric.*

Some children can make their own templates out of thin card, for themselves and others to try out. They should use a ruler where they intend to have straight lines, and make freehand curves carefully and smoothly. Point out that a simple shape without too many twists and turns in its outline will be easier to draw round and cut out.

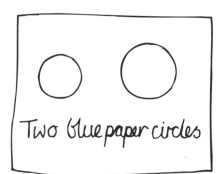

Recording
Staple or glue the shapes the children have made to large pieces of paper. Suggest the children write labels for their shapes, such as 'Two blue paper triangles', 'Two red fabric circles'.

Differentiation
Children:
- use a template to mark and cut out simple paper and fabric shapes
- use a template to mark and cut out a variety of paper and fabric shapes
- design a template out of card and use it accurately to make shapes out of paper and fabric.

Plenary
Discuss the shapes made by the children. Did they encounter any problems? Perhaps it was difficult to mark the fabric and that chalk or ballpoint pen might be more successful next time. Did the children find cutting the fabric rather tricky? Have they any tips to help others, for example about the way they held the scissors and fabric?

Display
Arrange the children's work for discussion and reference. Perhaps group the straight-line shapes and templates together to distinguish them from those with curved outlines. Alternatively, arrange the paper shapes separately from the fabric shapes. If the templates are collected together in a box near the wall display, the children can challenge each other to match template with shape: *Which template has Cassie used for her purple fabric shapes?*

ACTIVITY 3

JOINING TECHNIQUES

DESIGN & TECHNOLOGY

Learning objective
To practise and compare techniques when joining fabric.

Resources
Fabric, such as felt or other non-fraying material; paper; glue; stapler; thread; needles; plane shapes to use as templates, such as pairs (one large and one small) of squares or rectangles.

Preparation

Use the templates to cut three large and three small fabric squares. Decide how the session will be organised: you should introduce the activity and demonstrate to all the children, but they will need to practise the techniques in groups with an adult supervisor. Sew two pieces of fabric together as an example to show the children.

Activity

Talk about joining pieces of anything together. Show the children two pieces of paper. Ask how they would join them together. Make a list of their ideas, which might include using glue, sticky tape, paper clips, staples. If time allows, some of the suggestions could be tried out. Then ask the children how pieces of fabric could be joined. Are the same methods useful? Are there any other methods of joining fabric? Remind the children about their sewing and discuss how making stitches can join two pieces of fabric. Show the children the two pieces of fabric you have sewn together and suggest they examine their clothing to look for other examples.

Tell the children that they can practise three methods of joining fabric – using glue, staples and by stitching. First they must make shapes that can be fastened together. Show the children the templates you have used and the squares cut from the fabric. In turn, demonstrate how to fasten a small square onto the middle of the large one in three different ways – by gluing, stapling and sewing to achieve a picture frame effect.

In groups, give the children the opportunity to find two suitable templates, mark and cut out three of each shapes and join them together in different ways.

It might be appropriate to point out to the children that if pockets are made from two pieces of fabric, it is important to allow for the seam, particularly if an item of a certain size is to fit in the pocket. Some children can work together to produce a wall tidy with three pockets in which to store their spelling/note books. Each pocket can be joined to a large piece of fabric by a different method – gluing, stapling and sewing. Let the children evaluate the effectiveness of each method as they use the tidy.

Differentiation

Children:
■ with help, practise different methods of joining fabric
■ practise and compare techniques for joining pieces of fabric
■ demonstrate methods of joining fabric, understanding the need for a seam allowance.

Plenary

Ask the children to compare the joining techniques they have used. Which method did they find the easiest to do? Which do they think will be the strongest? Suggest that sometimes one method will be more suitable than another. In certain situations, sewing is more appropriate than gluing, for example, because it looks better and holds the join more firmly.

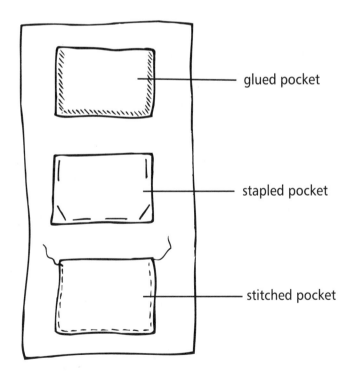

glued pocket

stapled pocket

stitched pocket

Display

Attach the children's examples of joining to card or strong paper. Suggest they label each method, perhaps also adding words or symbols to indicate which method they particularly enjoy doing, or which they find the most successful. Together, write a short explanation so that visitors understand the objectives of the activity.

Section 5

Making a puppet

FOCUS

DESIGN & TECHNOLOGY
- stages in making a puppet
- developing ideas
- considering design criteria
- making a mock-up
- creating basic shape and using finishing techniques
- evaluation

Preparation for section 5

The six activities in this section follow on progressively. They need to be completed in order as, in sequence, they guide the children towards making a finished product – a puppet. The children begin by looking for ideas, move on to planning their design, making a paper model, creating the puppet, adding the finishing details and finally evaluating their work.

ACTIVITY 1

LOOKING FOR IDEAS

DESIGN & TECHNOLOGY

Learning objective

To develop ideas for making a puppet by looking at a selection of ready-made puppets.

Resources

A selection of hand puppets; a video clip of puppets in action.

Preparation

Choose puppets that are simply made but provide contrasts in character and expressions and in methods of construction and finishing.

Activity

Show the children some fairly simple hand puppets. Explain that looking at finished puppets can provide ideas for making a puppet themselves. Elicit comments relating to the appeal of the puppet examples you have. Which one is a particular favourite? What is it that makes so many people like it? Is it the character it represents, its expression, the fabric it is made from, the unusual finishing touches? Talk about what makes each puppet different and interesting. Point out any features the children might like to use when creating their own puppet.

Ask the children who they think the puppets were made for. Are they all the same size? Perhaps some were made for smaller hands than others. Decide on a purpose for each of the puppets. Is there one that could be for a small child to entertain him or herself? Perhaps two or three puppets represent characters in a well-known story and could be worked by a group of children. There may be a character that is well known for presenting an important message to children, such as taking care on the roads or looking after the environment.

If appropriate, show a video clip of puppets performing to provide further examples and extend the children's ideas.

Next, look at the materials of the example puppets and discuss how the fabric and trimmings have been used to good effect. Talk about the faces, their expressions: whether the puppets are friendly, scary, happy or sad. How is this shown? Find out how many main pieces make up the puppets and how they are fastened together. Are the finishing details all attached in the same way? Are the puppet pieces sewn together or has glue been used?

Differentiation
Children:
■ examine puppets so as to develop ideas for designing
■ understand that examining puppets can provide ideas for their own designs
■ examine puppets, understanding how they can be useful when developing their own design ideas.

Plenary
Remind the children how useful it has been to examine examples of puppets. Point out some of the good ideas that might be used when the children come to make their own designs. Suggest the children begin to decide on the puppet they will make. Encourage them to talk to their parents/carers and older siblings about their ideas.

Display
Arrange the puppets informally so that they are available for the children to continue examining them while they begin to form their own ideas.

ACTIVITY 2

THINKING OF A DESIGN

DESIGN & TECHNOLOGY

Learning objective
To identify simple design criteria.

Resources
A selection of hand puppets; photocopiable page 48; pencils and crayons; board or flip chart.

Activity
Remind the children of the previous activity where they looked closely at a range of ready-made puppets to help them develop ideas for creating their own puppet. Briefly talk about characters, expressions, fabric and finishing details.

Then ask the children to begin to bring together their ideas for a design for making their own puppet. What sort of character would they like it to be? Ideas for characters can arise from class or school activities, from a favourite story, or perhaps related to the time of the year. Tell the children to think about the type and colour of fabric they will need for their puppet, and the materials they will require for the finishing touches.

Ask the children what makes a good puppet and what points they will need to consider when making their own design. Write up a simple list on the board that includes these criteria: the puppet will need to represent a particular character; it must fit the size of the hand of the person using the puppet; it will be made well and will not fall apart as it is used.

Suggest the children sit with their eyes closed for a few minutes while they think about their puppet design.

Recording
Ask the children to record their ideas by making a design plan using photocopiable page 48. Suggest they write notes to describe the character of their puppet and the materials they will

5

Making a
puppet

need to make it. Ask them to make a sketch to show how they expect the puppet to look, including the finishing details they will need to add. Point out the space on the sheet where they need to record the design criteria for making a good puppet. Remind them of the earlier discussion and encourage them to refer to the list compiled on the board.

ACTIVITY 3

A PAPER MODEL

DESIGN & TECHNOLOGY

Learning objective
To model ideas by making a paper mock-up.

Resources
Card; paper; pencils; scissors; glue.

Preparation
Make simple hand-puppet templates out of card. Make several of different sizes, perhaps small, medium and large so the children will need to make a decision as to which size they need. Mark lines to represent the seam allowance.

Activity
Explain to the children that it is useful to make a model of something before starting the real thing, a kind of trial run. This way, any mistakes or potential problems can be spotted early and materials are not wasted if things go wrong. Point out that artists and designers often make models or mock-ups to try out their ideas before starting on any project.

Tell the children that they can make a paper mock-up of their puppet in order to try out their ideas. Show them the different sizes of templates you have made of the basic puppet shape. Explain that it is important to choose the correct size for the hand that will be operating the puppet. Point out the lines which represent the sewing line or the space allowed for gluing and explain that the template used needs to be slightly bigger than the hand to allow for this joining process. If appropriate, demonstrate by drawing around a child's hand and cutting out two paper shapes, gluing them together and trying to fit in the child's hand.

Ask a child to draw around one of the templates to obtain two identical shapes. Cut these out and demonstrate how to fit and then glue them together. Let some children try the paper mock-up for size.

Give the children the opportunity to make their own mock-ups, choosing the correct size of template, gluing the shapes together and checking that the size is right.

Differentiation
Children:
■ use a template to cut out identical paper shapes and, with help, glue the shapes together to make a mock-up of a puppet
■ select a suitably sized template, cut out identical paper shapes and glue them together to make a mock-up of a puppet
■ understand why making a model of ideas is useful and, with confidence, make a paper mock-up of a puppet.

Plenary
Decide if the paper models were generally successful. Are the children happy with the size they have chosen? Remind them that if changes need to be made, fabric has not been wasted. The mock-up allows any problems to be resolved at this stage.

ACTIVITY 4

MAKING THE PUPPET SHAPE

DESIGN & TECHNOLOGY

Learning objective
To mark, cut out and join fabric pieces to make a basic puppet shape.

Resources
Templates from the previous activity; completed photocopiable page 48; photocopiable page 49; non-fraying fabric; pencils and chalks; scissors; large-eyed needles; thread; glue; pins; resealable bags in which to keep work in progress.

Preparation
Cut rectangles of fabric just slightly larger than the templates. Decide on the organisation of the sessions: all children will need to take part in the introduction and see the demonstration; while working on their puppets, children need to be in small groups with an adult supervisor. Decide which children will glue and which will sew the fabric. These groups can have separate demonstrations. More than one session will be needed for the children to complete their puppets.

Activity
Tell the children that now they have designed their puppet, practised the techniques they will need to use, and made a paper model, they are quite ready to begin making their puppet. Show them photocopiable page 49 and read through the instructions, demonstrating the steps one by one.
1. Find the right size of template. Show how to test a template for size by asking a child to place a hand on it. The hand should fit inside the dotted line that represents the seam allowance.
2. Choose two pieces of fabric. Remind the children that the fabric chosen relates to their design plan on photocopiable page 48. Point out that you have already cut the fabric into suitable pieces to minimise waste.
3. Draw round the template on each piece of fabric. Emphasise the importance of taking care and marking the fabric accurately. Ask for any tips the children might have to help each other. Perhaps in pairs the children can take turns, one to hold the template still while the other marks the fabric.
4. Cut out each fabric shape. Point out the importance of carefully cutting, using the scissors sensibly and safely. Again, ask for tips on ways of holding the fabric and cutting techniques.
5. Join fabric shapes together. Talk to the children about their sewing practice. Remind them of the seam allowance and the importance of starting and finishing properly. If necessary, draw guidelines on the fabric for the children to follow when stitching and show how pins can be used to hold the fabric together while the sewing takes place.
For children who are gluing, give a separate demonstration.
  In groups, with an adult supervisor, the children can proceed. Encourage them to follow the instructions step by step, ticking the small box as they have achieved each stage. At the end of the session, show the children how to attach the needle to their work safely. Ask them to store their puppet outline in a resealable plastic bag together with their plan.

5

Making a
puppet

Differentiation

Children:

■ with help, mark and cut fabric shapes, joining the pieces by gluing

■ with help where necessary, follow instructions and mark, cut out and use previously learned sewing techniques to join fabric pieces

■ work independently, following instructions to mark, cut out and join fabric pieces by sewing.

Plenary

Discuss the children's achievements. Ask if they had any problems. Was the sewing or gluing difficult? Did it take longer than they expected? Did they have to do any part again? Are they satisfied with their work so far?

ACTIVITY 5

FINISHING OFF

DESIGN & TECHNOLOGY

Learning objective

To use appropriate finishing techniques.

Resources

The children's work in progress; hand puppets from the display; scraps of non-fraying and other fabrics, including glittery, furry pieces and so on; braid; buttons; sequins; wool; needles; thread; glue; staplers; pins.

Preparation

Make the finishing materials available so that the children can easily find what they require. Plan the organisation of the sessions: ideally, children should work in groups with an adult supervisor.

Activity

Ask the children to refer to their plan to remind them what finishing materials they will need for their puppet. Discuss how they will be attached. Will gluing be the best method? Sometimes sewing might be a stronger, more suitable method? Perhaps stapling will be successful? Look again at the example puppets from the display and use their details to prompt discussion on the finishing techniques that will be used on the children's puppets. How will eyes be represented? What will be used to make a puppet look happy or sad?

  As the children work, give specific advice and guidance, perhaps marking positions where features need to be attached, pinning trimmings in position and so on. Encourage the children to try a range of methods of attaching the different features.

Differentiation

Children:

■ complete their puppet by selecting and attaching materials to apply finishing touches

■ complete their puppet by attaching appropriate materials in different ways to demonstrate a range of finishing techniques

■ select and apply appropriate finishing techniques to complete their puppet imaginatively and successfully.

Plenary

Arrange all the puppets for a general inspection. Admire the variety. Comment on the efforts that have produced the puppets.

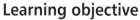

ACTIVITY 6

EVALUATION

DESIGN & TECHNOLOGY

Making a
puppet

Learning objective
To evaluate against design criteria.

Resources
The recently completed puppets and the plans; paper; pencils and crayons.

© 2003/Ian McKinnell/Alamy.com

Activity
Once the children have had a chance to admire their finished puppets as a group, let individuals evaluate their own work. Remind the children about the design criteria and the plans that they have followed.

Ask questions and make suggestions to establish if the puppet is the correct fit for their hand. Does it feel comfortable? If it is tight, perhaps it should have been made bigger. If it falls off easily, perhaps it should have been made smaller. Was the right template used? Perhaps the template itself needs altering before being used again.

Is the puppet well made? Are the seams joined firmly? Do the children think the joining method they used – gluing or stitching – was suitable? Are the stitches too big? Are there any holes? Discuss the fabric used. Was it right for the job? Was it easy to handle and cut? Would they have preferred a different fabric, a thinner or thicker type?

Encourage the children to examine the finishing techniques. Were embellishments fastened on properly? Is the puppet made to survive lots of use? Does it look how they wanted it to?

In pairs, ask the children to explain the character of their puppets to each other. Suggest they consider if the finishing touches were right for the character. Does it look like the character it is meant to be? Is the expression correct and recognisable? Would it be improved by any other additions? Encourage the children to exchange ideas constructively, perhaps using the puppets to communicate with each other. Suggest the puppets introduce themselves to each other, and describe their character, explaining why they look like they do. The children could rehearse a short dialogue between the puppets to show off their characters to a different pair of children or the rest of the class. Which puppets do the children think are particularly successful? Which ones make them laugh or frighten them? Which could be used to entertain a baby or be grouped together to make up a story?

Tell the children you want them to introduce their puppets to their parents. In pairs, let them practise introductions so that they can perform confidently when they take their puppets home.

Recording
Ask the children to describe their puppet by writing and drawing. Encourage them to write about the aspect of the puppet they are most pleased with and make a note of anything they think could have been improved. They could describe the puppet's characteristics in more detail and perhaps explain how it could be used in a performance.

Differentiation
Children:
■ talk about how they made their puppet and how they think it has turned out
■ discuss and write about their finished puppet, identifying any successes and problems encountered
■ talk and write about how well their puppet works in relation to simple design criteria.

Display
Display the children's puppets, perhaps with their plans and/or descriptions, to let the children appreciate their own and each other's work.

Thinking of a design

My puppet's character

What I will need

My design

What makes a good puppet

Making the puppet shape

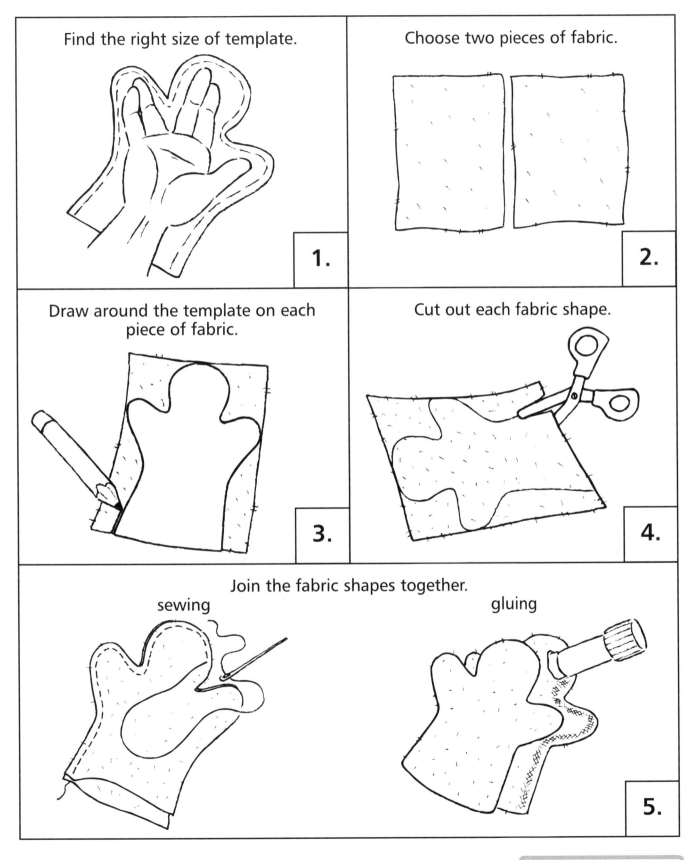

Find the right size of template.

1.

Choose two pieces of fabric.

2.

Draw around the template on each piece of fabric.

3.

Cut out each fabric shape.

4.

Join the fabric shapes together.

sewing

gluing

5.

SCHOLASTIC

Dance

FOCUS

PE

■ how bodies feel when still and at rest
■ exploring movement ideas relating to toys
■ moving confidently and safely, with changes of speed, level and direction
■ creating movement phrases using a range of actions and body parts
■ creating a simple dance
■ practising movement phrases
■ performing and evaluating a dance sequence
■ talking about dance ideas

Preparation for section 6

Check out the area where the dance activities will take place. This could be the school hall or other large floor space. Find out if the area is available on a regular basis to ensure continuity of the activities. Ensure the area is safe and the floor clean.

Decide where the children will change and store their clothes before and after the activities. Find out about any religious requirements relating to clothing and undressing. Be aware of any mobility or health problems and make appropriate arrangements. Refer to the school's PE policy relating to dance activities.

Inform parents about the procedures for PE, and dance in particular. Stress the importance of suitable clothing on the appropriate day. Show the children where to store their kit and encourage them to take the responsibility of looking after their own belongings.

Make sure that the children are fully aware of the procedures relating to dance activities. Talk to them about warming up and cooling down and tell them there will be time for such exercises within each session. Explain the purpose of the activities – that they will be working towards a performance of a dance they have created for themselves and will be exercising their bodies in an enjoyable way at the same time. Point out that there will be time to think, to practise sequences and to watch others. Remind them that they should be prepared to act sensibly with controlled movements and be aware that others are moving around them.

The activities in this section are progressive and should be followed in order. Ideas are developed and movements practised, culminating in a final performance and evaluation. Activity 1 can take place out of doors or in the classroom if space allows and provides a reference for appropriate times during other activities. Activity 7 is a non-physical activity that provides opportunity for the children to describe their dances and begin the evaluation process. The rest of the activities require a large space for the movement sequences.

Make time for the plenary sessions once the children have changed their clothes after the practical part of the dance activity.

It is important that the children find the dance activities enjoyable and perform primarily for themselves. However, depending on the confidence of the children and the time available, their achievements can be shown as a special performance to parents or other classes.

PE

INTRODUCTORY MOVEMENTS

Dance

Learning objective
To recognise how bodies feel when still and at rest.

Resources
Mats or soft area.

Preparation
This is a short activity separate from the main sequence of dance activities that follow and could be performed outdoors or within a carpeted area of a classroom. Only half of the class needs to be active at the same time, and it is important to refer to the learning objective on several occasions during the rest of the dance sessions so that the children have other opportunities to consider how their bodies feel. This activity could be used when a short space of time is available and the children are in need of physical exercise.

Activity
Ask half of the children to sit where they can observe the activity of the rest. Explain that they need to watch carefully to see what happens as the first group performs some dance exercises; then they will have a turn.

Start with some simple warming up activities. Ask the children, while sitting on the floor, to wriggle their fingers and thumbs, then to circle their hands by moving their wrists, first in one direction and then in the other. Then they should wriggle their toes and circle their feet by moving their ankles in both directions.

Next, ask the children to stand with their legs a little distance apart and feet fixed firmly on the ground. Encourage them to stretch their upper body by raising their arms, reaching sideways and bending over at the waist. If space allows, they can then lie down and exercise their lower halves by stretching their legs in all directions.

Finally, make suggestions for more vigorous activity. The children could practise, for example, jogging on the spot, working up to a running pace for a short while.

Ask this group to rest, while you ask the spectators if they have noticed any changes in the bodies of the children who have exercised. The resting group should notice that the others are out of breath and look hot. Ask the exercisers how they feel. They will recognise that their hearts are beating faster. Ask them each to feel where their heart is with their hand. Explain that their bodies had to work harder because they were moving more. They needed more breath, and breathing becomes deeper and quicker as the lungs are working harder too.

Ask the resting group how they feel. They should be cool, breathing normally and have regular heartbeats. Remind this group that their bodies have not yet worked hard.

Change the groups over and repeat the activity.

Again, ask the exercisers how they feel. The resting group can try to feel their heartbeats and notice their more gentle breathing compared with when they were exercising.

6

Dance

Differentiation
Children:
■ recognise that they feel out of breath when exercising
■ compare the differences in how they feel when exercising and at rest
■ compare how their bodies feel when exercising and at rest, and explain why their heartbeats change.

Plenary
Remind the children that their bodies need to work hard for some of the time everyday. This can be when exercising and dancing. When this makes them feel out of breath and their hearts are beating faster, their bodies are keeping fit and getting stronger.

ACTIVITY 2

PE

MOVING LIKE TOYS

Learning objective
To explore movement ideas relating to toys.

Resources
A small selection of old and new toys to act as stimuli for the children's ideas (a soft toy doll or clown; a clockwork animal; a small soft toy, such as a mouse or guinea pig); percussion instruments, such as a small drum and tambourine.

Preparation
Before the dance session itself, talk to the children about some familiar toys and about the toys they have looked at in the activities in sections 1 and 3. Consider the toys' characters and the movements the toys might make. Look at the soft toy clown. Demonstrate its floppiness, how it might walk, tumble and perform.
Compare this with the stiff movement of the clockwork toy animal. Then ask the children to describe how a small creature like a mouse might travel along.

Activity
Point out to the children that they need to get all parts of their bodies working after sitting still in the classroom. Ask them to:
1. stretch hands and fingertips towards the ceiling
2. stretch hands out to either side of the body, wriggling fingers
3. stretch hands to the ceiling again, wriggling fingers and standing on tiptoes
4. lie on the floor, stretching hands above the head and pointing toes
5. stretch arms and legs out to make a star shape on the floor
6. raise arms and legs towards the ceiling and hold toes with hands.
Tell the children they will be trying some different ways of travelling across the floor.
  Ask them to walk slowly, then more quickly; then to move along by hopping, then by jumping.
  Show them the soft toy clown and remind them of the movements a floppy clown might make. Suggest they try a clown's fast, funny walk, followed by a slow version. Use a percussion instrument to signal the change from fast to slow and back again if this seems appropriate.
  Talk about the clown tumbling or collapsing onto the floor. Give the children the opportunity to practise a short sequence that includes a fast and slow walk with a controlled tumble.
  Describe or show a clockwork toy animal and ask the children to mimic its movement. Perhaps it sways from side to side, travels along in a stiff manner or very quickly and

smoothly, or alters its speed and direction. Encourage the children to move like a clockwork toy, changing speed and direction as they travel along.

Finally, show the children a toy small animal, for example a mouse, and ask them to copy its movement. Encourage them to travel along close to the ground for a short distance and then lie and stretch the whole of their bodies before moving on.

To finish the session, tell the children that the toys are getting tired and need to rest. Ask them to repeat the movements of just one of the toys and make the movements slower and slower until they are resting either on the floor or standing stiffly. Provide a commentary so that the children work as a group, gradually slowing down their movements together.

Throughout the session, give the children the opportunity to watch each other perform. Point out particularly good movements and use of the body, and sequences that relate to how the toys move.

Differentiation
Children:
■ explore and perform movement ideas
■ explore and perform movement ideas, carefully following instructions and suggestions
■ explore and perform movement ideas imaginatively and thoughtfully, considering instructions and suggestions.

Plenary
At the end of the session, talk to the children about the movements they have performed. Point out how they needed to think about what they were doing to create thoughtful and interesting dance patterns.

ACTIVITY 3

PUPPET MOVEMENTS (1)

PE

Learning objectives
To move confidently and safely, with changes of speed, level and direction; to recognise how their bodies feel when exercising.

Resources
Examples of puppets to inspire and stimulate the children's ideas, for example one that can represent slow movements, another bouncing movements, another twisting and turning movements; percussion instruments.

Preparation
Before the session, remind the children about puppets as toys. Ask the children how they are different from other toys like teddy bears and dolls. Talk about being able to manipulate and control the actions of a puppet to bring it to life and reveal its character. If appropriate, refer to activities in section 2.

Activity
Tell the children they will be performing some movements to get their bodies gradually warmed up and working. Ask them to:
1. make small jumps on the spot, feet barely leaving the ground
2. make larger jumps
3. make really big jumps, using arms to help them get higher
4. lie on their backs on the floor, making a star pattern with arms and legs stretched out
5. curl up, hugging their knees and making their bodies into a small ball shape.

6

Dance

After a particularly vigorous sequence of movements during this session, ask the children how their bodies have changed. Talk about being out of breath, breathing more quickly, feeling hot and sweaty, and experiencing a faster heartbeat. Remind the children of the observations they made in activity 1.

Remind the children of their toy movements and explain that today's movements will represent puppets.

Show or describe a puppet that will make slow movements close to the ground. Ask the children to find different ways of moving slowly along, close to the floor. Suggest that those who have discovered three different ways are particularly successful.

Tell the children that the next puppet moves by bouncing along. Ask the children to try a sequence that involves bounces or leaps with a short, quick, travelling movement to link the bounces.

Show and describe a puppet that twists and turns as it travels along. Encourage the children to move around the room making sudden twists and turns and changing direction as they go. Perhaps use a percussion instrument to control the changes in movement and direction. Emphasise how important it is to be aware of others in the room and to avoid any contact, and that their movements should be accurate and controlled.

Finally, ask the children to put together the three different movements they have practised, bringing first one puppet to life and then another. Use a different percussion sound to signal the change from one puppet sequence to another. Choose some children to hold up the appropriate puppet while the action takes place. Provide time for groups of children to see each other's dance sequences, noticing the changes in direction, speed and level of movement.

Finish with all the children enjoying a final performance for themselves.

To help the children to cool down, suggest each puppet performs a final movement: a last crawl, a finishing bounce, a swift change of direction, and ending slowly with twisting and turning then sinking to the floor, remaining there quietly for a few seconds.

Draw the children's attention to how they feel now after a short rest. Is their breathing back to normal, are their heartbeats slowing down? Are they beginning to feel cooler?

Differentiation
Children:
■ perform distinct movements safely; are aware of differences in their bodies when exercising
■ perform a range of movements safely and with increasing confidence, showing distinct changes in speed, level and direction; talk about changes to their bodies when exercising and when at rest
■ confidently perform a range of linked movements demonstrating changes in speed, level and direction; make comparisons between their bodies at rest and when exercising.

Plenary
Tell the children how much you enjoyed their performances. Stress how important it is to move about safely, avoiding bumping into others, while at the same time enjoying and concentrating on their dance. Ask the children to describe how they felt after vigorous movements. Talk about their heartbeats, body temperature and breathing patterns. Compare this with how they felt after a rest.

ACTIVITY 4

PUPPET MOVEMENTS (2)

PE

Dance

Learning objective
To compose and perform movement phrases using a range of actions and parts of the body.

Resources
Three contrasting puppets; a selection of toys; a percussion instrument; a camera.

Preparation
Select and give names to three puppets of contrasting characters, on which the children can focus when composing their movement sequences.

Before the activity, remind the children of the nature of a puppet – a toy that will do whatever its operator/puppet master makes it do. Similarly, when performing as puppets, the children can think of their dance as representing what they want the puppet to do. Ask the children to choose one of the puppets you have selected to focus on when performing during this session, or to choose one of the toys from the toy collection and base their puppet on that. Suggest to the children that they think about their chosen puppet and its movements while they are getting themselves ready for the session. Look for opportunities for the children to notice how their bodies feel after movement and at rest.

Activity
To warm up, start with the children lying on the floor imagining they are a puppet in a cupboard or box and ready to come to life. Tell them that the puppet must exercise and test all the parts of its body before it can dance.

1. Wriggle fingers.

2. Stretch out arms in all directions.

3. Sit up slowly.

4. Move head slowly from side to side, then up and down.

5. Stretch out legs and wriggle toes.

6. Jump up and shake all parts of the body.

Ask the children to focus on their chosen puppet and decide how it will travel around. What will its special travelling movement be? Perhaps it will move along with short steps or a crawling movement; perhaps it will bounce, twist and turn or sway from side to side.

Give the children a short time to explore various movements until they have discovered a few suitable travelling phrases. Give general advice and encouragement as appropriate, perhaps asking some children to demonstrate their ideas. Suggest the children use all of their bodies and include distinct slower and quicker parts in their dance. Advise them to imagine the puppet and how it would move all the time they are moving.

Next, ask the children to devise a movement that they think their puppet will like to do over and over again, something like a catchphrase that will fit between the travelling sequences. Again, the children will need time to experiment. Suggest they try to include high and low movements in this phrase. Give specific advice as needed and look out for good examples that can be demonstrated. Provide further time for perfecting this movement. Emphasise the importance of controlled, thoughtful movement.

Now it is time for the children to put their two movements together to make an interesting sequence, travelling and then stopping to perform their special puppet movement. A percussion instrument can be used to indicate the change. If appropriate, suggest to the children that they count in their heads while performing the travelling phrase. This may help them to develop a rhythm to their dance.

In turn, give half of the class the opportunity to watch the others perform. Photographs taken at this stage are useful when discussing performances.

Dance

If time allows, let the children enjoy a final performance for themselves.

To cool down, ask the children, in character as their puppets, to make slower and slower movements until the puppet is resting quietly on the floor.

Differentiation

Children:

■ devise and perform movements, using a puppet for inspiration
■ devise and link phrases of controlled movements appropriate to a chosen puppet
■ with thought and imagination, devise and perform a sequence of movement phrases appropriate to a chosen puppet.

Plenary

Tell the children that the puppet movements you most enjoyed watching were those where the performers had thought carefully about what they were going to do, had practised and remembered and moved sensibly around the room.

Display

Make a display of any photographs taken to help the children realise how they look when moving and for later reference and discussion. This can be added to as the dance progresses.

ACTIVITY 5

CREATING A DANCE

PE

Learning objective

To develop a simple dance, focusing on the beginning and middle sections.

Resources

Puppets and toys used in the previous activity; video and still cameras.

Preparation

Remind the children of the puppet sequences they performed in the previous activities. Suggest they try to remember what they did in preparation for this session and consider any small changes and improvements they would like to make.

Activity

Ask the children to practise some warming up activities they have done before. Then choose an individual who is working well and ask the rest of the children to copy his or her movements. Choose a few more examples so that all the children cover a range of body exercises and warm-ups.

First, give the children the chance to practise their puppet movements from Activity 4. Suggest that this can be the first part of a special puppet dance.

Then explain that today they will be creating an adventure for their puppet that will make up the middle part of the dance. Ask the children to close their eyes and imagine what sort of antics their puppet character would be involved in. If necessary, make some suggestions relating to the puppets used for inspiration. Tell the children to imagine a short scene in which their puppet has a happy, sad or scary experience. How will he or she react? What will happen next?

Give the children some time to work out and test their ideas. Encourage deliberate, controlled movements, and give specific advice where ideas are lacking. Ensure the children move carefully, with consideration for the rest of the class.

Pick out some examples for the children to watch, either one child at a time or several children working at once. Make comments that will help all the children: *We know that Dan's puppet is happy because of the jolly, friendly movements and his smile. Eva's movements are scary and slow and her expression makes us a little frightened*. Afterwards, give the children further practise time of their own.

Suggest the children perform the travelling sequence again, which will be the beginning of their dance, moving on to the adventure, the middle part. Take photographs and video film of the performances, particularly the new, adventure sequence.

To cool down, tell the children that the puppets become tired and move slowly until they are resting quietly on the floor.

Differentiation

Children:

■ with help, combine movements reflecting dance ideas, using different parts of their bodies

■ choose appropriate movements for different dance ideas, putting these together as a dance sequence

■ explore more complicated combinations of movements fluently, putting together a controlled dance sequence.

Plenary

Tell the children how well their dances are progressing and that they should try to remember the beginning sequence and the middle part. Show the video film and point out any successful movements. Suggest the children practise at home, which will help them to remember the dance as well as improve their movements.

ACTIVITY 6

PE

THE WHOLE DANCE

Learning objective

To practise movement phrases and perform a dance with a beginning, a middle and an end.

Resources

The puppets and toys used in previous activities; video and still cameras.

Preparation

Remind the children to practise and think about their sequences from the previous sessions.

Activity

For the warm-up activities, choose children in turn to be leaders who demonstrate simple body movements. Making suggestions as appropriate: *Now we need someone to show us how to warm up our legs/arms/whole body*.

Remind the children that they are close to completing a whole puppet dance sequence. The beginning and the middle have been created and now an ending is needed. Encourage the children to think of a good idea for a special ending. It could be quiet and slow; sudden; perhaps with a big jump, a twist or a gradual fading movement. Encourage the children to

6

Dance

think of a movement or phrase that relates to their puppet and the practised parts of the dance. Give the children time to try out their ideas and then practise their ending.

Explain that now is the time to put the whole dance together. Tell the children that it might be useful, however, to have a special movement to link the three parts, which will help the performers as well as those watching. Suggest some links that could involve, for example, a twirl, a roll or a movement where the whole body is used, such as a stretch. Point out that a dramatic pause when holding an interesting position could be the right sort of link. Encourage the children to think of the link as a percussion sound, such as when a drum sounds or a bell rings.

Provide some time for the whole dance to be practised. Help those children who forget their sequence of ideas, perhaps clapping and counting softly when they should change from one part of their dance to another or commentating quietly to help them progress through their sequence.

Watch some of the dances as a class when the children feel confident enough to perform. Point out successful movements and praise or advise on a particular part of the dance, for example *Tom has a really good middle section, but he needs to make the ending more special*. Take photographs and video footage, which will be useful for evaluation.

Differentiation
Children:
- with guidance, put together and improve movement phrases to create a dance
- practise and remember patterns of movements to create a dance
- practise a dance with linked beginning, middle and end sequences, including thoughtful and imaginative movements.

Plenary
Tell the children that they are close to performing their completed dance. Remind them that they have devised a beginning, a middle and an ending and these parts are linked by a special movement or posture. Encourage them to practise at home before the last session, which will help them to remember the whole sequence. If appropriate, watch the video film of the children's dance sequences and ask them to notice good techniques and skilful movements as well as areas that may need a little bit more improvement.

It might be appropriate to ask a child to explain their dance before watching their performance. Otherwise, ask other children watching the video to say what they think is happening in a dance. Are the movements easy to interpret? Draw attention to different moods in the dances. Compare a lively, funny dance with a gentle, flowing interpretation.

ACTIVITY 7

MY PUPPET DANCE

PE

Learning objective
To describe and evaluate dance ideas and performances.

Resources
The puppets and toys from previous activities; photographs and video film of the children practising; paper; pencils and crayons; board or flip chart.

Preparation
Choose an appropriate time for this non-movement activity, perhaps when the children need time to consider their ideas or remember the sequence of their dance. Write out a vocabulary list of 'dance' words on the board, to include: *bounce, sway, jump, crawl, on the spot, beginning, middle, end, fast, slow, high, low* and so on.

Activity

Talk about the puppets and the dance ideas the children have devised and practised over a number of sessions. Point out how the puppets have been used as a focus to inspire ideas. Compare the different characters of the puppets and refer to the particular, contrasting movements that have come to be associated with them.

Remind the children that their dances have a certain sequence and, although they might make small changes and improvements, once the dance has been created, the pattern should be the same. Therefore, remembering what they have done from one session to another is important.

Show the video clips and photographs and help the children to recognise controlled and well-thought-out movements in the dances. Ask them to identify particularly good movement patterns. Which movements did they find exciting? Which slow sections did they think were especially good? Did any dancer use a pause effectively? Is there anyone's whole dance they would enjoy watching again? Use this opportunity to reinforce vocabulary on parts of the body and body actions.

Ask the children what they have learned from watching each other's dances. Could they use any of the ideas to improve their own performance? Suggest they practise further at home to improve their dance and enjoy this method of exercising their bodies.

Recording

Ask the children to describe their special dance. Prompt them to mention the puppet that gave them ideas for their movements. They can explain the type of movements they have chosen for each part of the dance and the linking movements. Ask them also to write about their favourite part of the dance, noting if they are especially pleased with any particular movement or phrase. Point out the vocabulary list and encourage the children to refer to these while writing. Do they think they need more practice or are they ready for the final performance? If appropriate, children can draw themselves engaged in a particular movement of the dance.

Differentiation

Children:
- describe their dance sequence with words and drawings, recognising good movement patterns
- provide an explanation of their dance sequence using words and drawings; point out good movement patterns and recognise where improvements can be made
- show understanding of how to create a dance sequence by describing their ideas and movements in sentences and drawings; understand the importance of evaluation and recognise where improvements can be made.

Plenary

Read out some of the children's descriptions and explanations. Emphasise the need for thinking and remembering so that the dance is improved with every practice.

PE

ACTIVITY 8

THE PERFORMANCE

Learning objective

To perform a dance sequence.

Resources

The puppets and toys from previous activities; video and still cameras.

6

Dance

Preparation
Alert the children to the day of their special performance. Tell them that there will be some practice time at the beginning of the session.

Activity
Suggest the children decide on their own warm-up activities in preparation for the performance. Give general encouragement if necessary.

Then allow the children time for a last practice. Provide specific guidance as necessary, reminding anyone who has forgotten parts of their routine, as well as encouraging those who are less confident.

Depending on the number of children and the time available, in turn, ask about a half or a third of the class to perform while the rest form the audience. It might be appropriate to encourage a particularly confident child to perform alone. Insist on complete attention from the audience and thank and applaud the performers when they have completed their dances.

Take photographs and video film of the performances.

When everyone has had the opportunity to show off their dance, make suitable comments on the children's achievements.

Differentiation
Children:
■ remember practised movement sequences and perform a dance
■ remember dance sequences and perform movements expressively to reflect ideas
■ remember a sequence and perform it confidently and with expression, showing clear understanding of the idea of a dance sequence.

Plenary
Look at any photographs and video footage you have taken and admire the puppet dances. Comment on particularly successful movements, children who have remembered their sequences, those who have performed imaginatively and expressively, any special efforts and achievements. Compare earlier photographs and look for improvements in posture and expression. Refer to the enjoyment of performing and talk about the effects on the body of exercising and resting.

Display
Organise the photographs into a special display to highlight the children's achievements. It may be appropriate to display them in the hall where performances take place or within the classroom with the puppets and toys.

Display
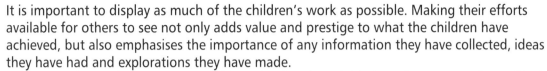

It is important to display as much of the children's work as possible. Making their efforts available for others to see not only adds value and prestige to what the children have achieved, but also emphasises the importance of any information they have collected, ideas they have had and explorations they have made.

  If children know that their work will be valued and available for others to see, they will take more care over presentation, and at this stage the habit of always producing their best efforts is encouraged.

Individual presentation

Collect each child's individual 'paper' work – drawings, completed worksheets, written pieces, plans and so on – and present them in a folder or as a booklet, which they can personalise and show to each other and their parents. As there will be samples of sewing and other examples of design and technology techniques practised, incorporate a pocket to contain these. If necessary, any pieces of work needed for classroom display can be photocopied for the children.

  Provide photocopies of pictures or photographs, such as interesting old and new toys, a museum display, a scene from a puppet performance, which the children can add to their work to give their booklets or folders an extra dimension. Let the children include copies of photographs of themselves practising and performing their puppet dance.

Classroom display

Begin to build up a display as soon as the work on *Toys* begins. The display will evolve over the weeks as the work progresses.

  It can be useful to display each child's work relating to any specific activity in a temporary way, perhaps with Blu-Tack, so that discussion and evaluation can take place and the work can be admired. At this stage, make sure the work is displayed on a level where it can easily be seen by all the children. Where appropriate, photocopy and enlarge examples of individuals' work to use with a particular display.

  If space is limited in the classroom, extend the display into the corridor or school hall. The hall will be a particularly appropriate area in which to display any photographs of the dance sequences if the physical activities have taken place there.

  Frequently refer to the displays as the topic develops, reminding the children of the different elements of their work and the progress they are making, and making links and connections across topics.

  The activities in *Toys* lend themselves to two distinct but connected areas of display: 'All kinds of toys' and 'Puppets'. There are opportunities for particular types of display: incorporate the children's work when setting up a class toy museum and create a workshop section of the room for storing and displaying the work relating to practising techniques and designing and making.

Display

Suggestions for display for each section
All kinds of toys
■ Allocate a suitable temporary space where the children can safely display their own toys that they have brought to class relating to the first activity. Then use a selection of classroom toys to form a display, together with the children's work about their favourite toys. Provide opportunities for sorting and re-sorting the new toys with appropriate labels and headings. Extend this display to include toys from the past as the activities proceed. Label all the toys and make sure the children know which ones they are allowed to handle and play with and which ones are only for looking at. Put similar old and new toys side by side with informative labels so that comparisons can easily be made.
■ Display the toys' adventures the children have devised and their drawings of old toys, and include any photographs relating to a museum trip or visiting expert arising from activity 5.

Puppets
Create a special puppet display with as many different types of puppets as possible. Again, indicate which puppets the children can handle and explore and which are to be left for observing and special demonstrations. Arrange the children's work from this section together with pictures of puppet characters and puppet shows.

Displaying toys
Begin to develop the display from section 1 into the class toy museum. Add the children's work comparing old and new toys, and the information they have acquired to accompany the exhibits. Make a space available for the time sequence and other exhibits according to how they have been sorted. Incorporate ideas the children have seen at a museum or from pictures of similar displays. Raise the profile of the toy museum by inviting other classes, parents and visitors to view the exhibits. Taking turns, the children can keep the exhibits tidy, make sure everything is labelled, decide on opening times, provide tickets, act as guides and so on.

New techniques and Making a puppet
■ Create a workshop area while the activities of sections 4 and 5 are in progress. Arrange and label materials and tools with any appropriate instructions as to their use. The children's efforts with sewing, using templates and joining materials should be displayed close by. If wall space is limited use boxes to file the work, which can be removed when required. Store the children's plans and mock-ups in the workshop where they will be easily accessible to the children. Make sure the children are familiar with safety and organisational routines and procedures when they are making their puppets. Provide informative labels to explain the children's achievements to visitors.
■ The finished puppets can be arranged close to the puppet display from section 2, together with the children's descriptions and evaluations of their work.

Dance
Photographs of the children practising and performing can be used as part of the puppet display or they could be mounted, labelled and arranged separately with the children's descriptions of their movement ideas. Build up the display as the activities progress and refer to the photographs for evaluation.

Assessment

At the end of the topic *Toys*:

HISTORY
■ Can the children describe artefacts and communicate the information to others?
■ Are they aware that old toys can tell us about the past?
■ Can they recognise similarities and differences between old and new toys?
■ Are they able to decide on categories for sorting toys?
■ Do they understand how museum displays can tell us about the past?
■ Can the children recognise the importance of arranging artefacts in a time sequence?
■ Do they ask and answer questions about toys in the past?
■ Can they communicate what they have discovered by speaking, drawing and writing, and through a display of artefacts?

DESIGN & TECHNOLOGY
■ Are the children aware that there are different kinds of puppets?
■ Can they identify the parts and uses of a puppet making clear labelled diagrams?
■ Can they use basic sewing techniques?
■ Can they use a template for marking and cutting out identical pieces?
■ Have they practised basic joining techniques and discussed their advantages and disadvantages?
■ Can the children generate their own design ideas according to simple criteria?
■ Do they understand the importance of making a paper model to try out their ideas?
■ Can they apply newly learned techniques to a designing and making task?
■ Can they mark, cut out, join and finish and evaluate their design task?
■ Can they use new vocabulary as appropriate?

PE
■ Do the children respond to stimuli when considering dance ideas?
■ Can they copy movements and follow instructions?
■ Can they talk about their dance ideas with descriptive language?
■ Can they devise movements which reflect the moods and feelings of their dance ideas?
■ Do they move confidently and safely in a controlled manner?
■ Are the children aware of the differences in how their bodies feel when exercising and when at rest?
■ Can they create and remember a dance sequence which links a beginning, a middle and an end?
■ Do they perform with a sense of expression and rhythm?

Drawing the topic to a close

Look back with the children over the work they have done during *Toys* and highlight any special incidents and achievements. Point out how much they have learned and the range of their achievements. Remind them of any visits they have made, experts they have met and investigations they have taken part in. Comment on the new techniques they have learned that have helped them design and make their own puppet. Remind them of how well they created, remembered and performed their dances. Ask what aspect of the topic they have enjoyed the most.

Celebrate the children's successes displayed in the museum and bring out any other work and photographs you may have removed to make room for subsequent displays. Talk about the children's achievements here and in the dance performances and ensure that all the children feel proud of their work. Point out the valuable help parents and carers have given, especially those adults who have helped with classroom tasks.

Organise a special event as a finale. Perhaps hold a special open day of the toy museum with the children designing programmes, which can be printed using appropriate software. Suggest the children act as guides providing information about the exhibits. If the children are sufficiently confident, arrange an extra performance of the dance sequences. Invite other classes and/or parents and carers.

To demonstrate their puppets, the children could devise a simple entertainment sketch for each other or as part of a performance during school assembly. The puppets could perform a simple story or perhaps deliver a message, such as ways of keeping safe during the holidays, caring for pets or looking after the environment.